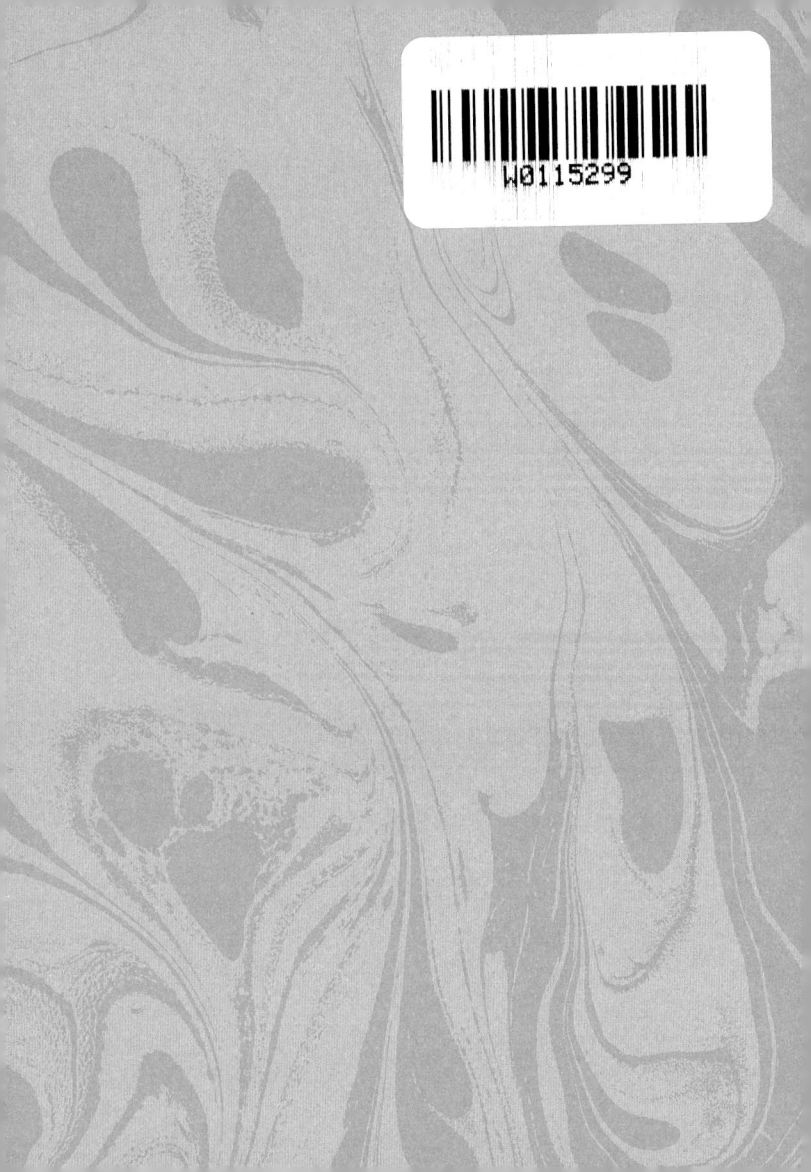

MOON MAGIC

LUNAR RITUALS
and
SPELLS

✦ ◆ ✦

GAIA ELLIOT

Quadrille

PART I

✦

PART II

✦

The Magic of Intention

New Moon Intentions

Full Moon Intentions

PART

· I ·

'THE MOON IS THE FIRST MILESTONE
ON THE ROAD TO THE STARS.'

— Arthur C. Clarke

Introduction

The relationship between the Earth, moon and sun forms the basis of our daily life. The Earth takes 365 days to orbit the sun, while the moon takes around 27.3 to orbit the Earth, with about 29.5 days between one full moon and the next. Understanding the relationship we have to the moon, as well as its effect on nature and our universe, provides valuable insights about its energy and power, which we can use to our advantage.

This is the magic of the moon – and it shouldn't be underestimated.

For example, the moon exerts a gravitational pull on the ocean's tides, and because our bodies are around 60 per cent water, there's reason to believe that we too might be responsive to the moon's energy. This could explain in part its magnetic pull on our dreams and imaginations, which encourages creative exploration in our lives. That the universe should supply us with such energy is very much to our advantage when it comes to setting new or full moon intentions, and working with the rituals and spells we use in setting them.

The moon's gift to us is that we learn by reflection. Whether you are new to this understanding or already an advocate, you can take your own power deeper and further by working in conjunction with the moon's energy. Using rituals and spells, it becomes possible to access this magic.

7

Moon Mythology

The moon is considered a female deity, with the lunar cycle reflecting the monthly female fertility cycle. This potential creativity embodied in the female finds itself celebrated in a number of goddesses.

8

SELENE

Sister to the Greek god Helios, who personifies the sun, Selene's Roman identity is Luna, and her gift is to grant serenity. A focus on her during your new or full moon spells is particularly useful if you are in need of a period of restorative rest.

HECATE

This torch-bearing goddess is linked to the light of the moon, and offers a powerful connection to fertility and childbirth. If you are using a full moon ritual to focus on any maternal concerns, hers is a useful energy to include.

ARTEMIS

The twin to the Greek sun god Apollo, Artemis is the daughter of Zeus. Her Roman identity is Diana, goddess of the moon and a huntress. Artemis is good to focus on when you need to re-energise and increase your physical strength.

9

PHOEBE

Grandmother to Artemis and Hecate,
she embodies the full moon and is the
culmination of all female power. She also
has the gift of prophecy, so can be a useful
focus for those lunar spells and rituals
where you are in search of an answer
to a particular question.

CHANG'E

Having drunk from the elixir of eternal life,
Chinese mythology says that Chang'e was
saved from her husband's, the legendary
archer Hou Yi, wrath by being transported
to the moon for safety. When you need to
feel secure about your sense of purpose, this
moon goddess is a good focus.

10

CERRIDWEN

A moon goddess from Celtic mythology, Cerridwen is also considered a witch. From her cauldron, she can elicit wisdom and spiritual insights. A positive force, she embodies change and rebirth, a useful transition on which to focus in times of uncertainty.

DARK MOON LILITH

In Hebrew mythology, Lilith was created from dust to be Adam's first wife, but she rebelled and left the garden of Eden. She represents our deepest, most hidden desires, and her influence helps us access our independence and personal strength, giving us the energy to realise our true potential.

11

The Moon and its Astrological Signs

During the lunar cycle, the moon moves through the 12 astrological signs of the zodiac, spending around 2.5 days in each sign. It is useful to know the current astrological weather in which you are working, particularly in relation to your own natal chart. When we talk about 'astrological weather' it's a reference to astrological influence. Whether the sun is currently in Taurus or, say, Scorpio, there is a subtle astrological influence in the air that is relevant to whichever of the 12 sun signs is currently in play. With regard to the moon, the astrological 'weather' changes around every 2.5 days rather than 28. It provides additional insight into the particular energies currently in play at the time of asking your question. The energy when the sun is in Taurus will be subtly different to that in Pisces or Gemini, as the ruling planets' energy – in these cases Venus, Neptune and Mercury – have quite specific characteristics. Likewise, when the

12

moon is in a particular sign, this too can have a resonance. The characteristics of each sign create what's termed astrological 'weather', exerting their influence over the phases of the moon (see pages 16–17), peaking at the new moon and full moon. A new moon in Scorpio creates quite different 'weather' to a new moon in Leo, for example. Because of this, it's always worth checking what you are working with when you set your new or full moon intention, and using this knowledge as part of your ritual or spell-casting.

It's also worth noting where the moon falls in your own astrological chart, as this can also power up its effects. So if your natal moon is in Sagittarius, then when either a new or full moon is also in this sign, it will be valuable to you in setting your intentions.

Finally, there's a moment when the moon moves between one sign and the next, and this is when it's referred to as 'void of (its) course'. When this occurs, there can be a temporary void, a pause in the energy around you. It can be brief, a matter of minutes, but it can last several hours or days. When this happens, it can provide a hiatus in energy, which is often experienced as a benign stasis, an opportunity to take stock. Wait it out and reflect on the moment; the universe has got your back and all will be well again, once the void has passed.

13

Moon
Phases

The phases of the moon are important in terms of their power, and knowing where you are in the lunar cycle can be helpful, even if you are only concentrating on new or full moons for the purpose of setting intentions, rituals and spells.

Each phase of the moon has its own energy, and that energy will also be influenced by its astrological weather (see page 12). For example, waxing crescent moon in Pisces might be an excellent time for your imagination, which can be particularly useful when problem-solving. Likewise, a waning gibbous moon in grounded Capricorn might help your resolution to stay on track. It's easy to find out which astrological sign the moon is currently passing through online.

14

TIMING

Although we can work with the timing of the moon's phases, focusing in particular on the new and full moons to set our intentions, it's worth remembering that time is a modern construct designed to help us catch trains, and as such it can't be applied to the magic of the moon's energy. How this impacts on you, your intentions, and the rituals and spells you employ, is completely individual, and outcomes aren't always immediate. Be patient and keep faith with the universe's energy, trusting that its timing will be in your best interests and aligned to your higher purpose.

✦

LUNAR JOURNAL

Keeping a lunar journal can be really helpful in noting the circumstance of new and full moons, the astrological sign in which they fell, your own intentions and any outcomes. You can also keep a note of what rituals and spells you applied to enhance the lunar magic available to you and work in accordance with the energy of the universe.

PHASE ONE: NEW MOON

Pause and reflect on where you are. Cleanse old energies. Plan and set intentions for the next lunar cycle. Always consider what the astrological weather is, what sign the moon is in and harness this energy to support you.

PHASE TWO: WAXING CRESCENT

As the level of reflected light from the moon increases, it will become easier to see in which direction you need to extend your energies.

PHASE THREE: FIRST QUARTER

With the moon's increasing light, take stock and see where your energy needs to be focused in order to continue to progress.

PHASE FOUR: WAXING GIBBOUS

Your commitment and excitement about the potential of your intention set at the new moon will become increasingly visible by the light of this almost-full moon.

PHASE FIVE: FULL MOON

Here you reach the peak energy of your intention. How is it working out? What do you need to focus on or discard?

16

PHASE SIX: WANING GIBBOUS

This phase provides a potent opportunity to refine your intended purpose, based on lessons learned.

PHASE SEVEN: THIRD QUARTER

The energy of this phase allows you to release and forgive, should there be a need. This does not just mean forgiving other people; be generous to yourself about your own failings too.

PHASE EIGHT: WANING CRESCENT

This phase sees the end of the lunar cycle and a moment of darkness just prior to renewal. It offers an opportunity for reflection and contemplation.

LUNAR ECLIPSES

A lunar eclipse is a potent event. The moon's reflected light will be temporarily dark, obscuring what can be seen. It can take some time for its impact to play out, but an eclipse always brings a blast of energy to facilitate change. It is worth noting in which astrological sign an eclipsed moon occurs, because this too will be significant in how this energy plays out.

18

PART

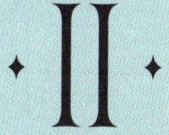

·II·

The Magic of Intention

New and full moon rituals and spells are all about setting your intention for the next lunar cycle. Your intention should be in your best interests and should aways align to your higher purpose, so it's worth meditating on these things prior to any new or full moon.

Keeping a record of your intentions can be useful, helping you to see when your intentions are met and progress is made. It will also help you to evaluate on where to focus your intentions next. Think of this as a work in progress – and remember that time is a modern construct (see page 15) and that things may not always happen exactly as or when you expect, but will instead occur in line with the universe's plan.

What follows are some suggestions about aspects of life, love, health, luck and money that are often the focus of new or full moon intentions. This will help you define where to direct your energies at any given time, using all you know about the moon's special magic and how you can access this twice a month.

Before each new or full moon spell or ritual, check which astrological sign the moon is in (see pages 12–13), as the current astrological weather will have an influence. You may choose to align your intentions with what is actively supported by that particular sign at a new or full moon. For example, setting your intention for love will be assisted by a moon in Taurus and Libra, whose ruling planet is Venus, goddess of love. For health, a moon in Virgo is good, while for luck, a moon in Sagittarius works well, as its ruling planet is the beneficial Jupiter.

23

ESSENTIAL OILS

Using essential oils in new or full moon rituals can also help focus energy. For example, to ground fiery energy when the moon is in Aries, Leo or Sagittarius use vetiver to calm an active body and mind. To lift earthy energy when the moon is in Taurus, Virgo or Capricorn use rosemary to stimulate mood and concentration. While to bolster watery energy when the moon is in Cancer, Scorpio or Pisces, use jasmine to uplift and energise, and to focus that airy energy when the moon is in Aquarius, Gemini or Libra, bergamot helps to relax and boost the mood.

24

CRYSTALS

Crystals have properties that resonate and help combat
negative energies. When it comes to creative and
cleansing rituals, particularly at the time of new or full
moons, using crystals can help enhance these. Using
your astrological birthstone can help strengthen and
focus your energy on specific intentions. Some crystals
are particularly aligned to the moon and the moonstone
is the most obvious, but also clear quartz, selenite,
amethyst, aventurine and rose quartz. Himalayan
salt (also a crystal) is a powerful tool to focus energy
and can be used alone or in rainwater to re-energise
other crystals.

25

WHAT YOU WILL NEED

For a new or full moon spell or ritual,
you will need the following:

a candle

an essential oil to help heighten your senses
and intuition (see page 24)

a pen and paper to record your intention;
you may decide to keep a journal (see page 15)

a crystal – perhaps your birth stone –
that has been energised either in sunlight
or moonlight (see page 25)

Before you start, meditate on your true intentions,
which should be positive and aligned with your
principles. You cannot set an intention that will bring
harm to another person; it has to be positive, otherwise
it could rebound badly on you. You don't want to put
out negative energy into the universe, so focus on the
good and allow the universe to redirect its power
back to you.

WHAT TO DO

For each ritual or spell, whether for
a new or full moon:

1

Light your candle and essential oil burner (if using).

2

Place your energised crystal in your dominant hand.

3

Meditate on your intention and make this a statement
of intent about what you wish to manifest at this point
of the lunar cycle. State it aloud.

4

Write it down in your lunar journal.

27

New Moon Intentions

A new moon is a new beginning. It also offers an opportunity for cleansing, so let go of those things that no longer serve you, and create space for new dreams, hopes and ambitions as they evolve, in alignment with your higher purpose. As the lunar cycle continues, each phase (see pages 16–17) yields its own illumination and energy, so there's always a continuation to the magic of your intention.

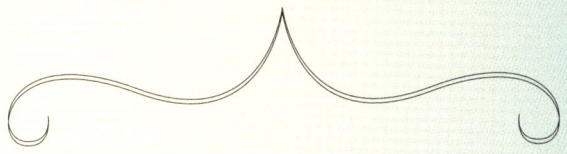

FOR LOVE

Love can be available to you in many forms,
but here we are talking about intimate love in
a personal relationship, the course of which
doesn't always run smooth. New moons are a
brilliant time to assess what you are prepared
to do for love and to reject what you won't do.
This is something about which it is worth
being very clear sighted, and the light of a
new moon can assist you here. Loving
yourself comes first, and that love should be
unconditional; what follows is based on that
and helps set parameters of equality and the
ability to receive love from others.

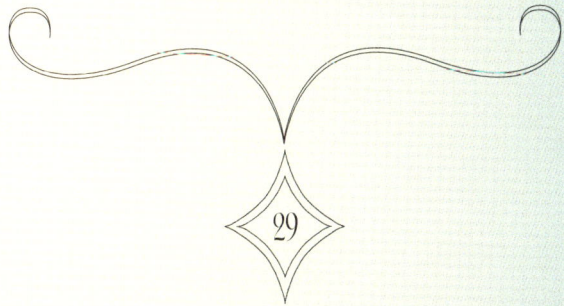

29

FOR
NEW LOVE

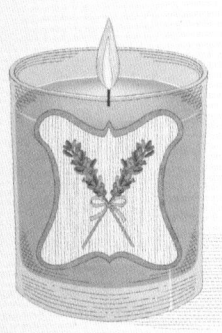

These can be heady days, and it is always
worth keeping one foot metaphorically
on the ground, even while the love
between you and another is cherished for
its own sake. Enjoy the pleasure you are
receiving, and focus your intent on
nurturing it.

I bring my best self
to this new love
and trust that it will
flourish.

FOR UNREQUITED LOVE

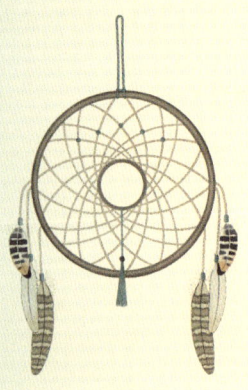

Challenge negative ideas you may hold about friendships. Believe in the value of good friendships and let go of limiting self-beliefs that may have prevented you from forming nourishing relationships in the past.

If it doesn't enhance
your life, it doesn't
belong in your life.

FOR
DWINDLING
LOVE

Your intimate relationship may be losing
its initial thrill; you may be drifting apart
through the forces of circumstance or a
change in attitude. If it's a love worth
preserving, it may need some work and
thoughtful input. Set your intention on
what you value in the relationship and
what needs fresh energy.

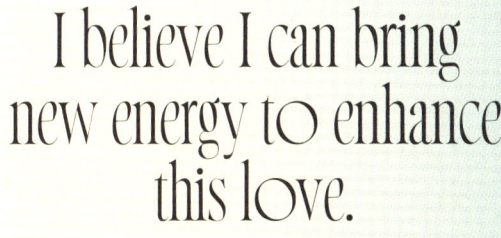

I believe I can bring
new energy to enhance
this love.

FOR
RECOVERY
FROM LOVE

Sometimes, even great love affairs can
burn out and leave you feeling distraught.
Remember that if you have loved once,
you have the capacity to love and be loved
again – this remains 100 per cent true.
Meditate on how to preserve what was of
value, and how to let the rest go.

I cherish the memory
of the good
I received to build on
in the future.

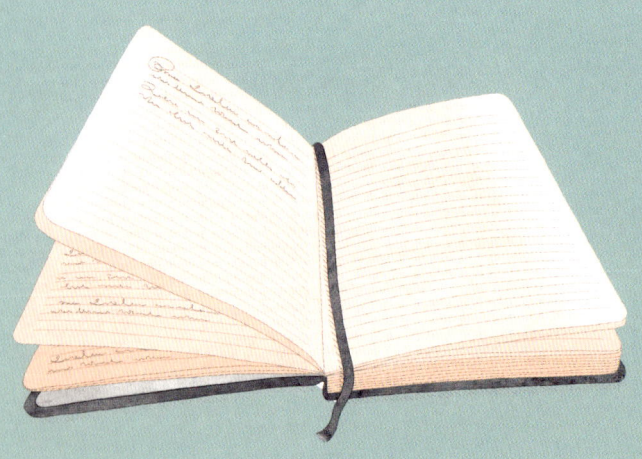

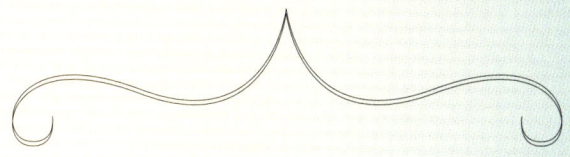

FOR MONEY

Money is a resource, something that has value in how it is made, saved and used. It's a commodity that allows us to do things such as taking care of others, travelling or buying a home. It is a form of security and a feature of life, but a desire for it shouldn't blind you to the needs of the soul, or the needs of others. Use the new moon's energy to express your gratitude for what you have and for that on which you want to build.

TO ATTRACT MORE MONEY

You need to consider how you earn an income, whether it's in service to others or yourself, as a member of a team or in isolation. Then look at what you are doing and how you are doing it, and focus your intention on maximising this.

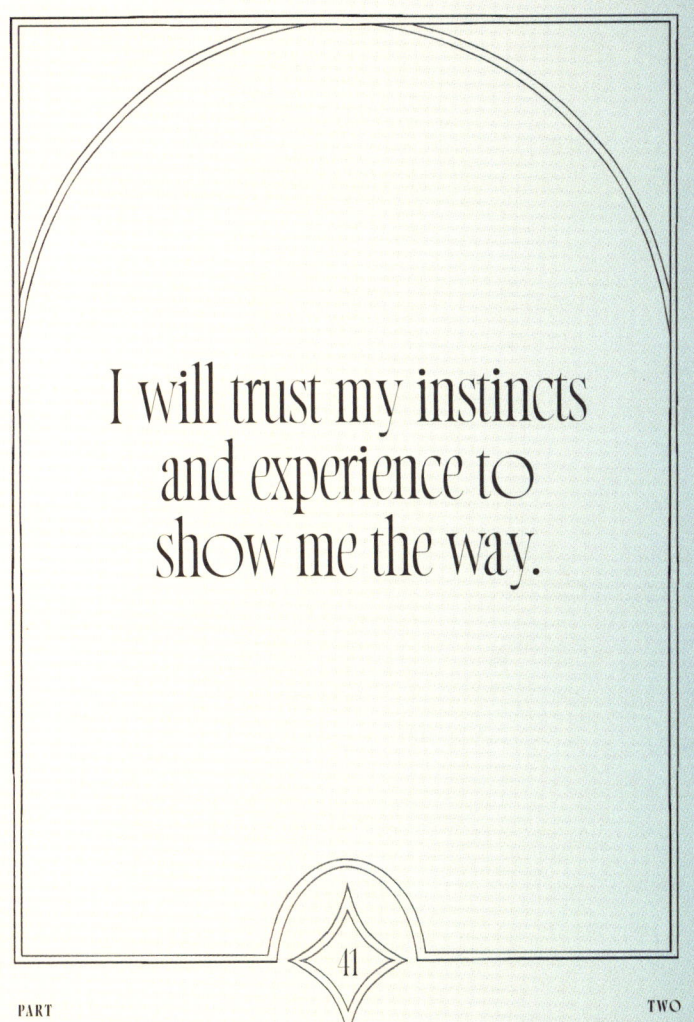

I will trust my instincts
and experience to
show me the way.

TO SAVE MONEY

You may have a reasonable income, but might not be sure how to enhance its abundance. A regular savings plan can help, but it takes some thought and organisation to find an approach that allows your savings to accrue without you feeling deprived. Set an intention that is aligned to your goals.

I will set my goals
according to my
means and in alignment
with my future.

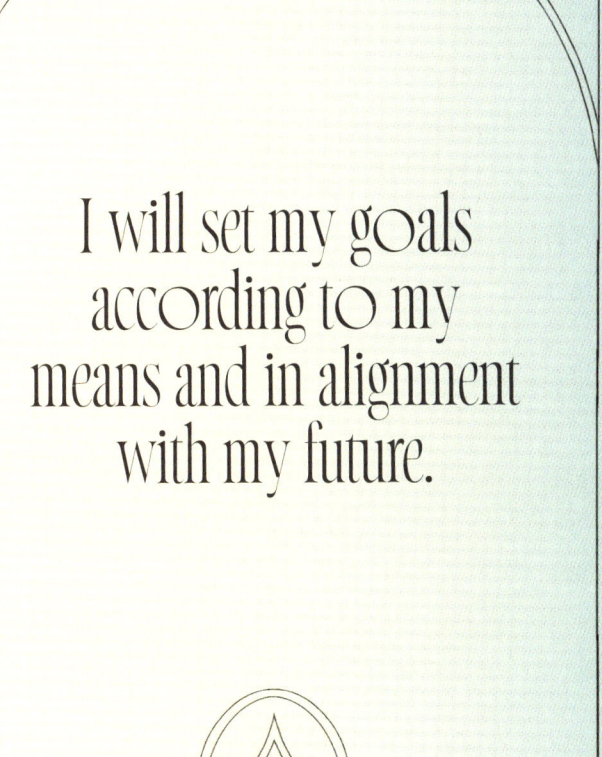

TO SPEND
MONEY WISELY

If you are to benefit from any material abundance that you have earned or been gifted, it makes sense to focus your intention on its wise use, to improve or enhance your life's experience and to have something to show for it.

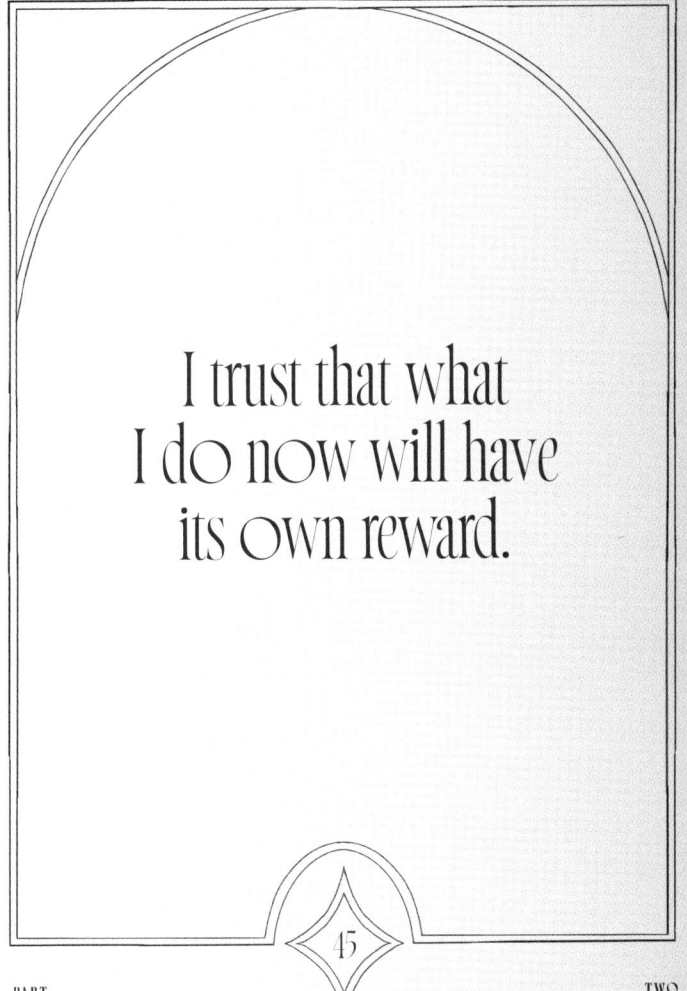

I trust that what
I do now will have
its own reward.

TO GIVE MONEY AWAY

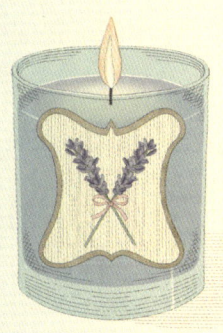

Sharing anything with the world
means that you trust in its abundance
and that you will never lack what you
need. Giving to others is the bedrock of
many belief systems, and opens up the
flow of exchange. You will only benefit
from this energy.

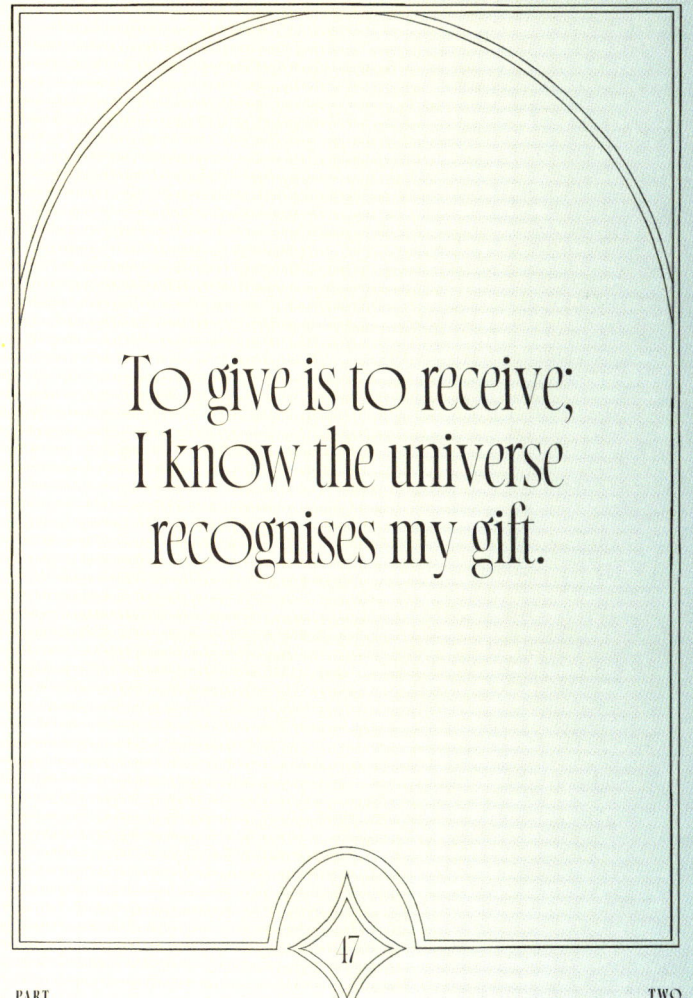

To give is to receive;
I know the universe
recognises my gift.

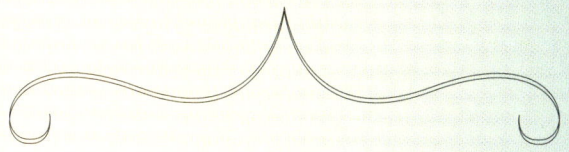

FOR LUCK

Luck is an interesting concept, because while it can seem outside our control, we are, in fact, capable of making our own luck, and very often do. Remember that, whatever the circumstances, you still have agency and can still make choices. Each new moon is a particularly potent opportunity to reassess what you can do to change your luck.

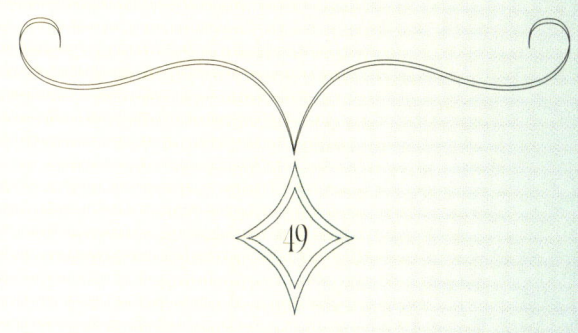

19

FOR IMMEDIATE LUCK

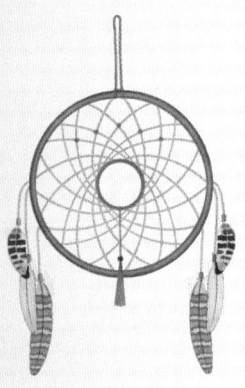

One way to enhance your luck is to practise gratitude. Once you've taken a look at the luck you've already been granted or the lucky breaks afforded you, then you can start to see how what you've done before can work for you again.

I can trust my hunches
to make my own luck.

FOR LUCK IN A PARTICULAR ENDEAVOUR

This is probably focused on a particular project or outcome, so the specific details are worth considering before you set your intention. Make a note of these and it will become clear where the energy of your intention needs to be directed.

I will make positivity my default to achieve my aims.

TO CHANGE YOUR LUCK

Sometimes we can try as hard as we like
to catch a break and nothing seems to
work. If what you've always done no
longer seems to work, change your
approach or attitude and do things
differently, then set your intention
based on that.

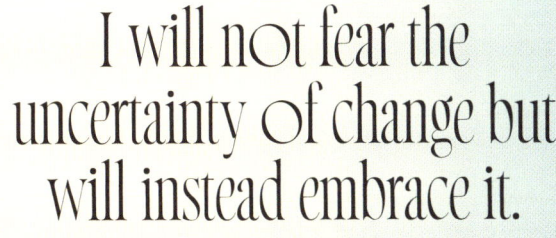

I will not fear the uncertainty of change but will instead embrace it.

TO ENHANCE YOUR LUCK

You consciously feel you're a lucky person, but there are times when your confidence dwindles and nothing seems to go quite right. When this happens, review those things that have brought you luck in the past and focus your intention on them.

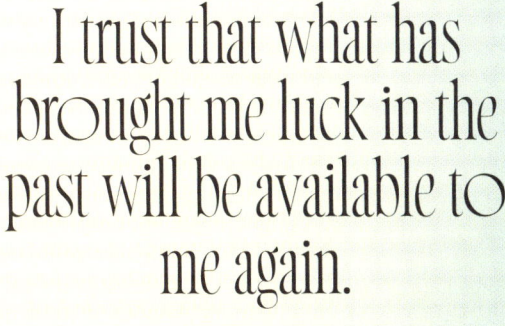

I trust that what has
brought me luck in the
past will be available to
me again.

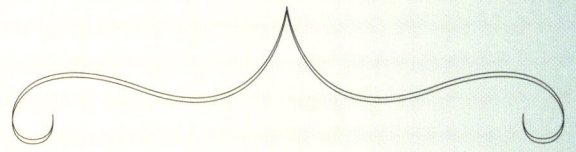

FOR HEALTH

Our physical and mental health
are both deeply important to our
happiness, and it is worth taking steps
to preserve them through the choices
we make and the way we live our lives.
A new moon is an opportunity to
honour this. If, for example, you
feel you need to rethink your
relationship to work, food, exercise
or sleep, then take the time to set the
intention of taking practical steps
to improve things.

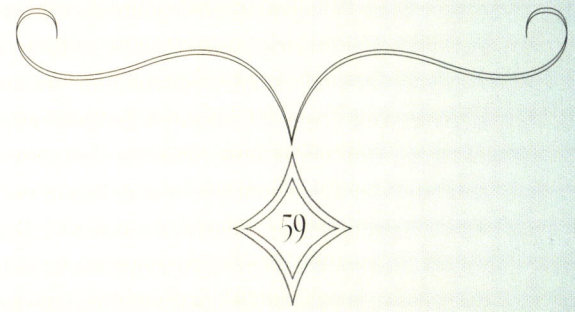

FOR AN IMMEDIATE HEALTH PROBLEM

✦ ✦

Whatever the problem, see it as an opportunity to change those things that contributed to it in the past, so that you can improve things now. This can take courage, and may mean asking for help.

I will trust the
universe to give me
the help I need.

FOR
IMPROVING
GENERAL HEALTH

There's a custom of setting New Year's
resolutions around health – resolutions
that often fail by February. But when
you've got a new moon every month, you
get an opportunity to set and reset your
intentions, focusing on what worked and
understanding how to stay on track.

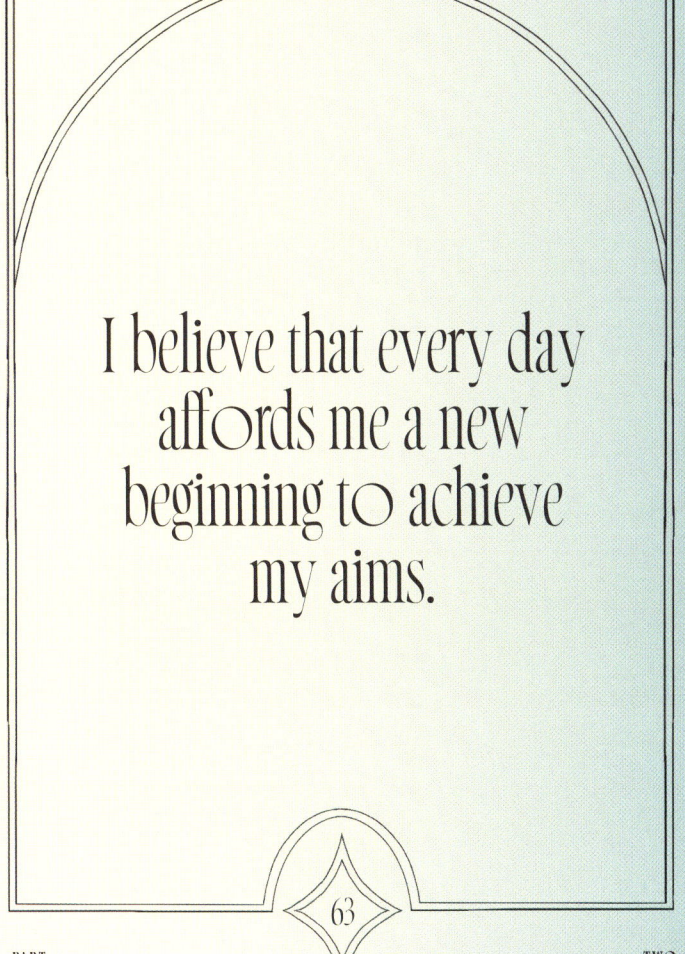

I believe that every day affords me a new beginning to achieve my aims.

✦ FOR GROUNDING ✦
MENTAL HEALTH

Mental health is as important as physical
health, and the two are closely linked.
You owe it to yourself to ensure you
develop resilience and avoid becoming
overwhelmed and burned out. Sometimes
this is as simple as learning to prioritise
your own needs.

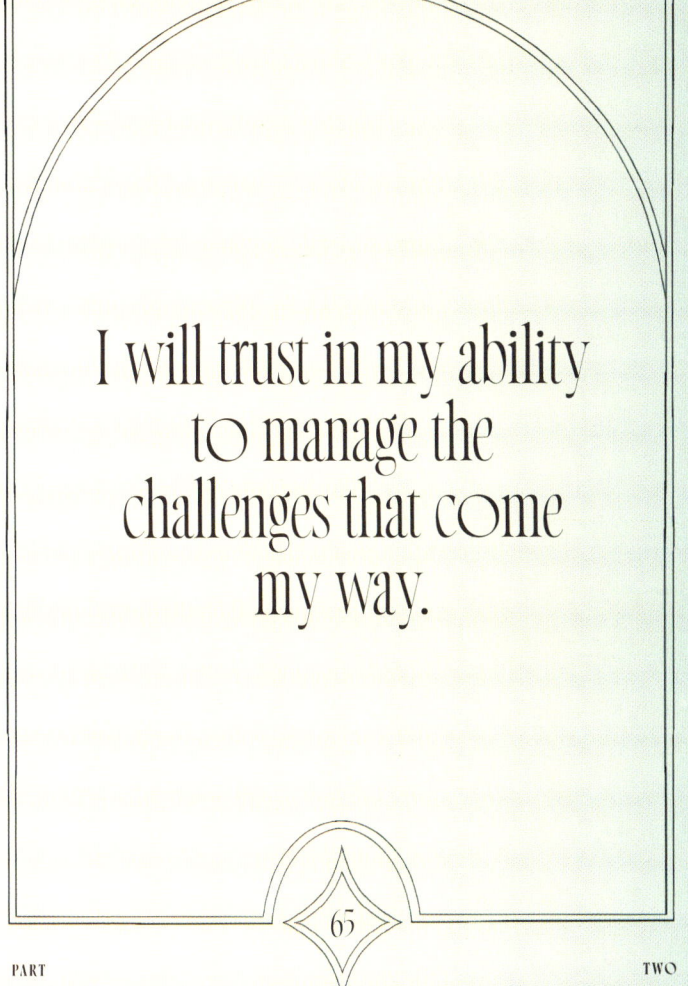

I will trust in my ability to manage the challenges that come my way.

FOR
RECOVERY
FROM ILLNESS

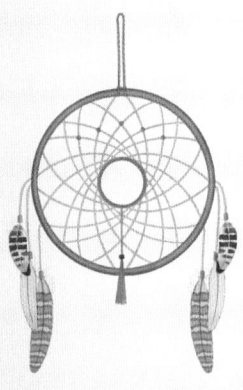

Convalescence is a serious business; it takes time, but it really pays off. If you need to recover your physical or mental health, it helps to understand this and to invest in what you need to do to ensure your complete recovery, such as rest or gentle exercise.

I will say no to those demands I can't meet, so that I can recover my health.

Full Moon Intentions

A full moon is often a time when you might see the culmination of the intentions you set at the new moon. It is a time of peak illumination, allowing you to review your new moon intentions and see what's working out and what you might need to review or discard. Your full moon intentions also benefit from the lunar cycle's peak energy, enabling you to power up your intentions at this time.

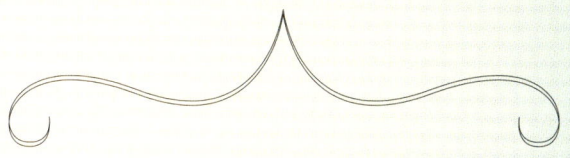

FOR LOVE

The romance of a full moon is there
in myth, literature and reality: its
beautiful light can help show us our
true feelings. Falling in love can
sometimes cloud our judgement, and
sometimes we seek to get our own
needs met while ignoring red flags.
Full moon energy can really help you
here, shining a light on your best
interests, even if it means hard
decisions are necessary.

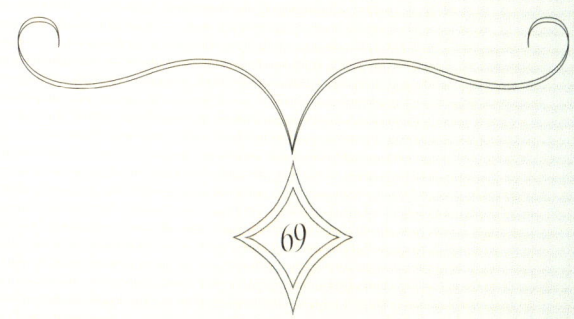

69

TO FIND OUT IF YOU ARE READY TO LOVE

This can be a big question, particularly after a heartbreak. A full moon helps you see the reality of a new situation: are you ready to trust again? Set your intention to answer this question to help manifest the right time for what you desire and deserve.

I practise self-love
in order to love
others.

TO FIND
OUT IF YOU
ARE READY TO COMMIT

A full moon can bring emotions to a head, and this can be helpful when you want to know if the timing is right for your next move. This may mean going exclusive, moving in together or even marrying; focus on identifying what's right for you.

I will trust the universe to guide me in making the next step in love.

WHEN
THINGS FEEL
STAGNANT

Sometimes our intimate relationships
seem to stall and a full moon can
illuminate what might be causing this.
Take this opportunity to focus on the
relationship's needs as well as your own,
and set an intention to get things back
on track.

I take responsibility to see and seek the best in this relationship.

WHEN YOU HAVE TO PART

✦ ✦

A full moon shines the greatest light on a situation and brings things to a head. You may be aware that change is necessary, but are not sure how to make this change or whether you have the courage you need to do so. Focus your intention on how to manage this.

I trust in my ability
to love again when
the time is right.

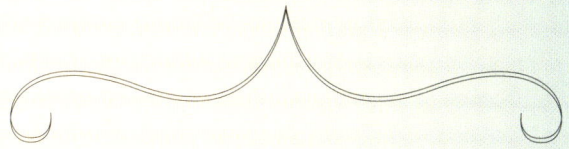

FOR MONEY

Our material needs are facilitated by money earned, saved or gifted. For most of us, this means we must find a way to earn a living that rewards us – and not just materially, although financial remuneration is a valid recognition of our talents, experience and expertise. Many find it difficult to ask for what they deserve in return for their graft; a full moon can help promote creativity, productivity and growth.

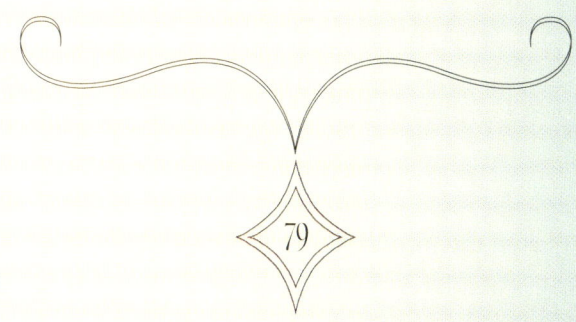

ASKING FOR WHAT YOU DESERVE

Many of us find this difficult. Use full moon energy to power your commitment to yourself and set your intention to improve your material income through your work, by focusing on your worth to your employer and sharing this with them.

With clear expectations, I can achieve this goal.

CAPITALISING ON YOUR TALENTS

✦   ✦

Looking at ways to extend and enhance your talents can improve your material income. Set your intention to develop that expertise, perhaps through further training or study; it will always pay off.

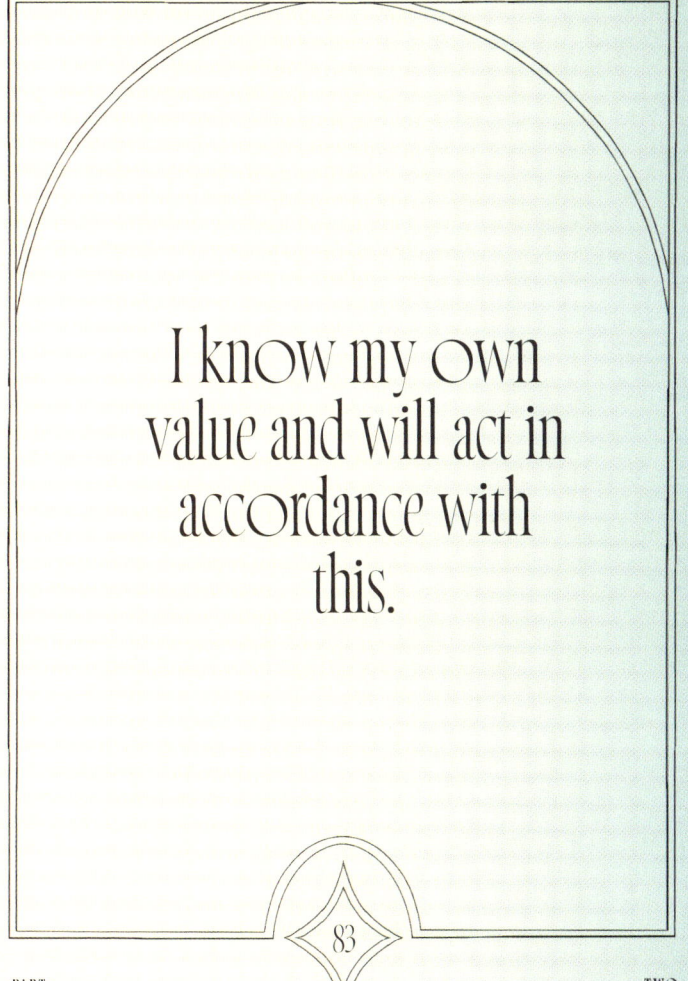

I know my own
value and will act in
accordance with
this.

83

TO FIND OUT
IF YOU ARE READY
TO COMMIT

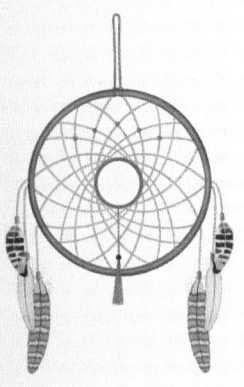

A full moon can bring emotions to a head, and this can be helpful when you want to know if the timing is right for your next move. This may mean going exclusive, moving in together or even marrying; focus on identifying what's right for you.

I will trust the
universe to guide me
in making the next
step in love.

MAKING
A CHANGE

✦   ✦

Sometimes it's just not possible to
increase our material income without
making a change. This might be a change
of job or a change of circumstance. A full
moon can help illuminate what change
you need to make, helping your set your
intention to achieve it.

I will trust in the
benefits of change,
and make change
happen.

✦ PAYING IT FORWARD ✦

Material wealth is a blessing, especially
when it affords you opportunities to pay
it forward, not just through money but
also often through time. Full moon
energy can help you see what difference
you can make by paying it forward.

I believe that the
universe will
answer my needs.

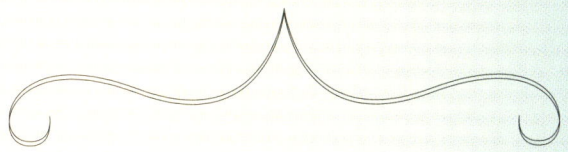

FOR LUCK

When you're looking for a lucky break and put your intention out there into the universe, you are on the first step towards manifesting the luck you desire and, through your efforts, deserve. Many people appear to benefit from luck, but it is often the result of their reactions to certain circumstances and the way they have contrived to make these circumstances work in their best interests. A full moon helps to illuminate how you can do the same, and receive the luck that you deserve.

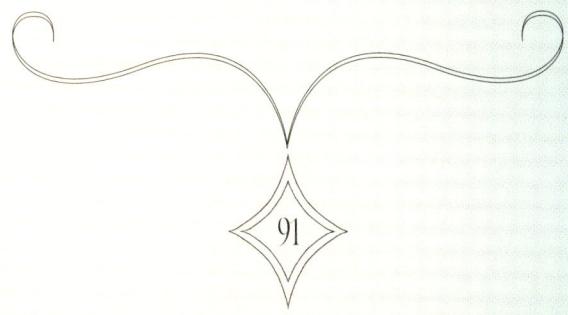

A LUCKY
BREAK

That chance event you want to make happen? The full moon's energies can step in here by helping you focus on how you can improve your chances of that lucky break. So meditate on that and set your intention accordingly.

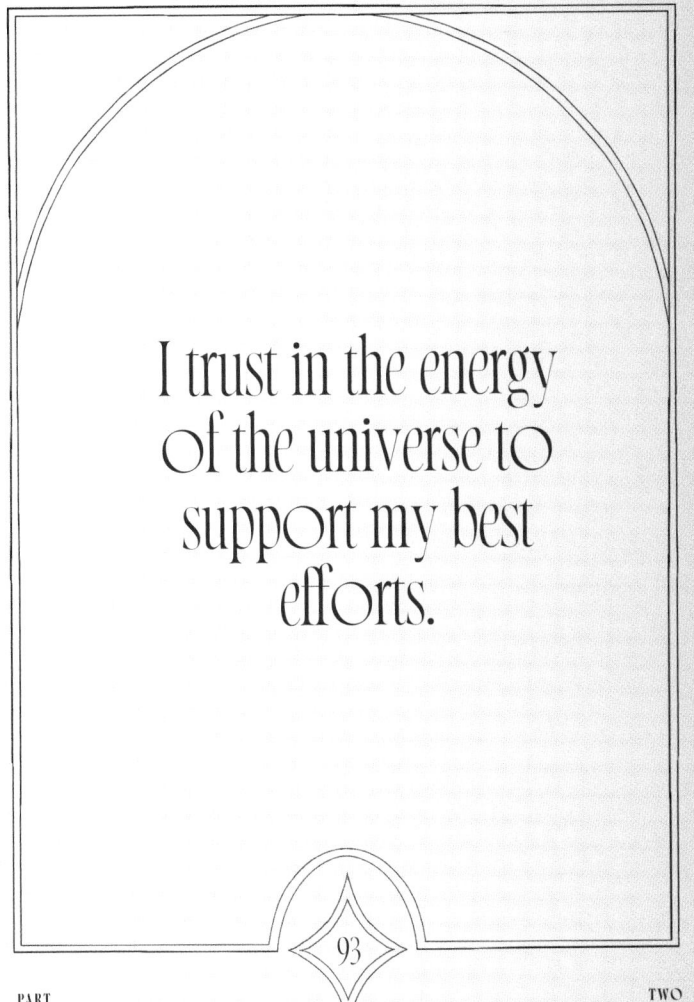

I trust in the energy
of the universe to
support my best
efforts.

✦ LOOK TO SUCCESS, ✦
NOT FAILURE

Luck isn't just down to random chance,
it's also a frame of mind. When you are
contemplating a scenario in which you
wish to succeed, visualise how you might
do this. Set your mindset with a full
moon intention that focuses on this.

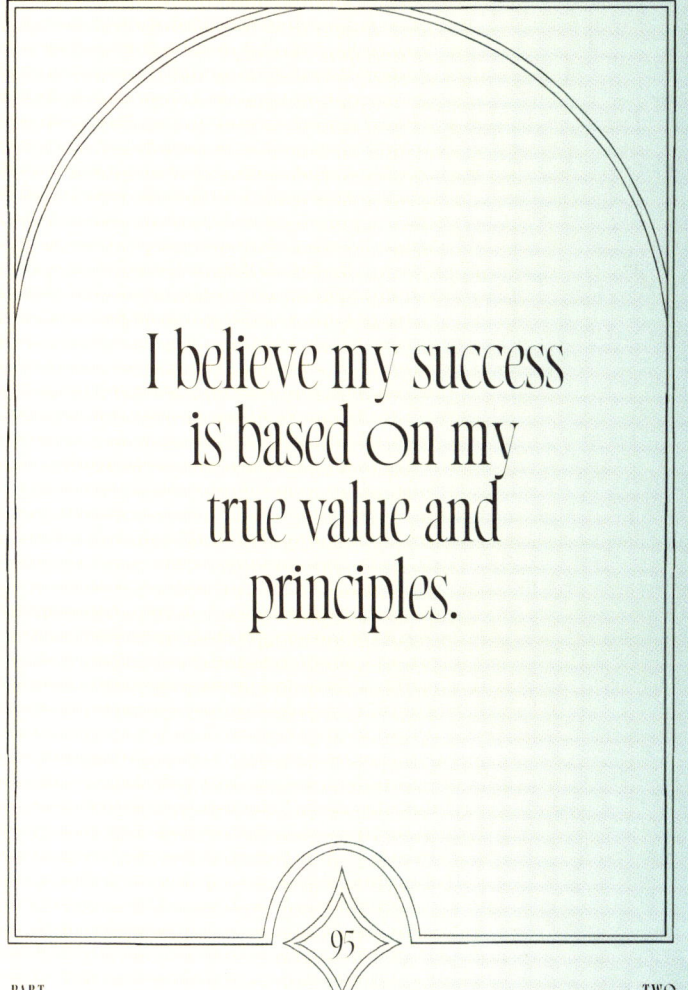

I believe my success
is based on my
true value and
principles.

ENDURING LUCK

Consider luck as a force for good. The universe is on your side and wants your life to align with your best efforts, so set your full moon intentions to align with your higher purpose and the universe will reward you.

Every day I will
look to the
wisdom of the
universe for the
luck it offers.

TRUST
YOUR LUCK

Lucky people seem to show an aptitude
for trusting their gut. Intuition about
what might work out for you can be
powered by full moon energy. Meditate
on what long- or short-term choices you
could make that might enhance
your luck.

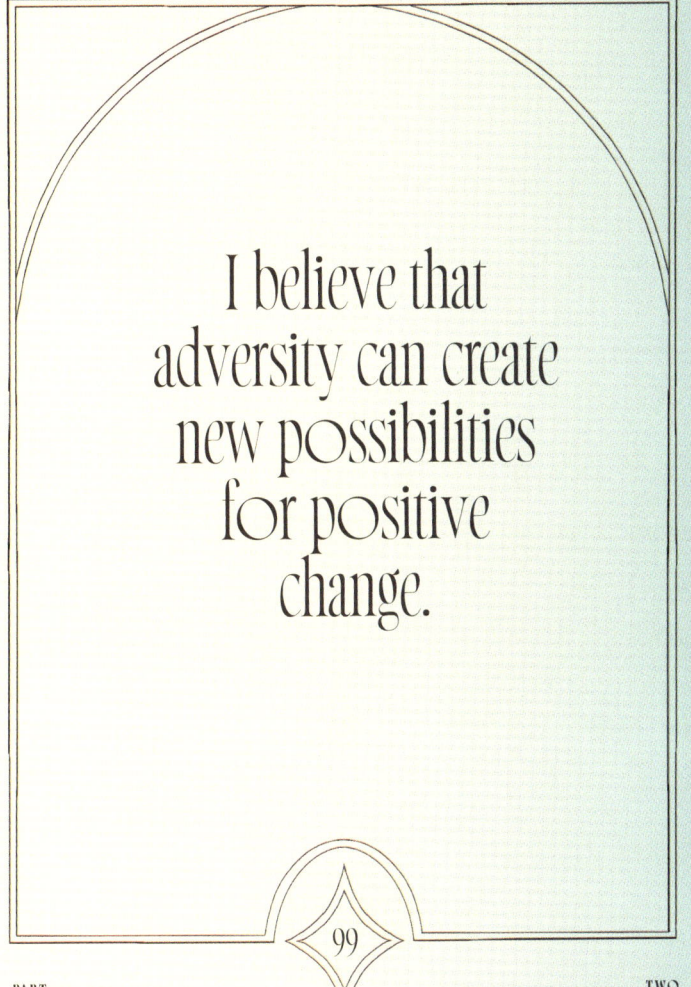

I believe that
adversity can create
new possibilities
for positive
change.

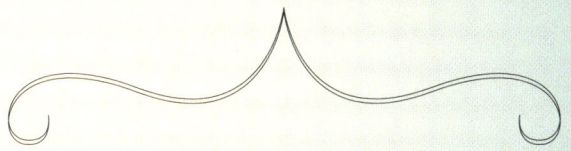

FOR HEALTH

Our physical and mental health are crucial facets when it comes to how we manage our lives. We can really benefit from a regular audit to check we are doing the best for ourselves, whatever our situation or circumstances. The cumulative power of a full moon is an ideal opportunity to focus on this, set our best intentions and ensure we stay on a positive health track.

101

MANIFEST
POSITIVE HEALTH

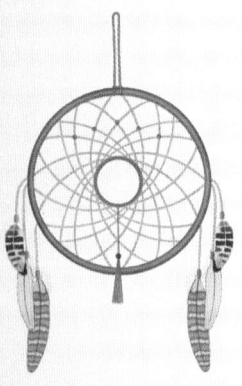

The energy of a full moon can help you kick-start ways to improve your health generally. This may mean adopting a better sleep regime, committing to regular exercise or making an effort to avoid processed foods.

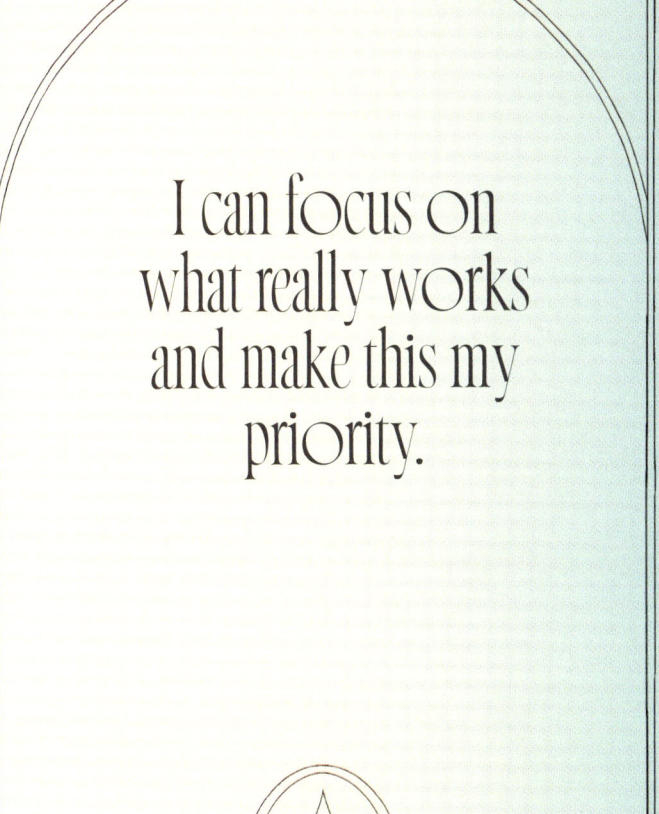

I can focus on
what really works
and make this my
priority.

103

RECOGNISE MENTAL HEALTH CHALLENGES

Use the full moon to cast light on areas where you may be struggling with your mental health, and focus your attention on managing these and improving your mood.

I will trust in
positive thoughts
and reject those
which are negative.

105

RESTORE
DEPLETED ENERGIES

After a sustained period of work, a bout
of illness or an injury, a full moon can
help you focus on recuperation, allowing
you to focus on a full recovery – which is
so necessary for a return to
strong energy.

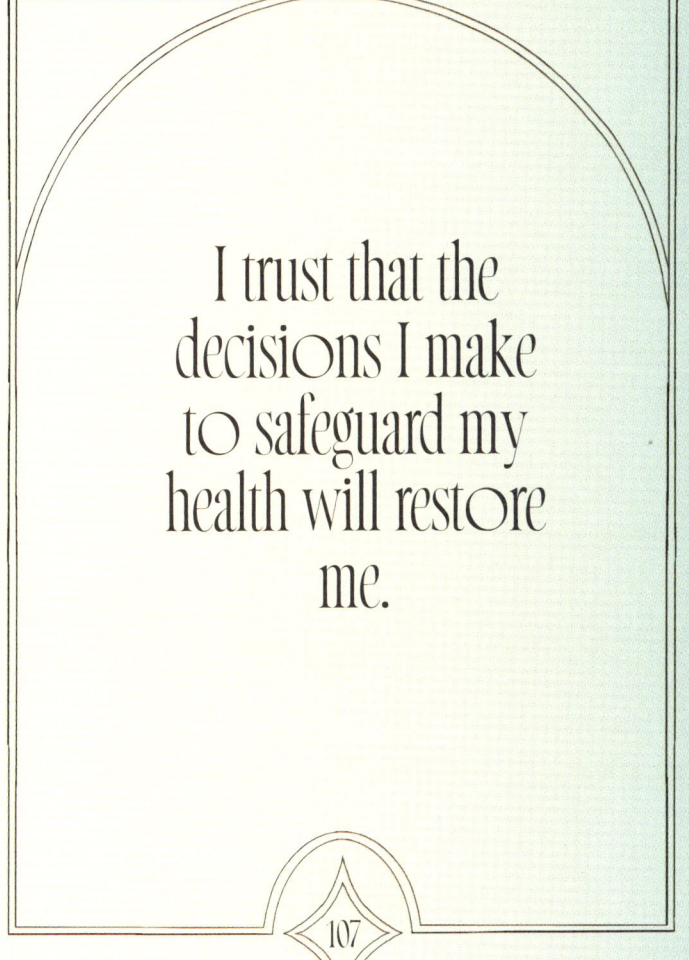

I trust that the
decisions I make
to safeguard my
health will restore
me.

GUARD
AGAINST BURNOUT

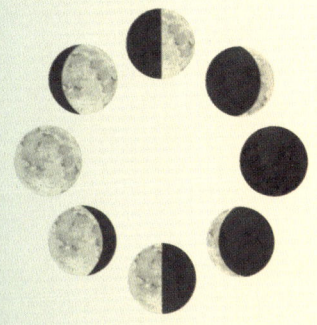

Use the full moon to help you
recognise those areas of stress that can
accumulate and eventually lead to
burnout. Pre-emptive changes can
make a big difference and help you take
steps to avoid it.

I believe that saying
no can sometimes
be an act of
survival.

Acknowledgements

First and foremost, thanks are due to my inspirational and creative publisher Kate Pollard, who is always willing to go the extra mile to produce books of substance and beauty, and to Phoebe Bath for her good humour and editorial skills. Thanks are also due to illustrator Lucy Pollard, and the the design team at Evi O. Studio for creating such a gorgeous series of books.

Thanks are also due to my teachers, past and present, who inspired me on my journey as an esoteric practitioner, enabling me to develop my own skills and talents. And to my Romany grandmother, who provided insights into a world beyond our immediate reality, and access to it.

Finally, to my family on this journey we call life: thank you for your support and love.

110

About the Author

Gaia Elliot is a green witch based in London. She loves tending to her garden and being surrounded by the abundance of nature, which feeds into her spell-casting and magic-making. Gaia believes that anyone can harness their inner power by tapping in to their intuition. She has a strong interest in tarot, the power of the moon and psychology. Gaia's spiritual journey started when she was a young woman, and she loves nothing more than helping other people to start or continue their own journeys. She is the author of *The Book of Answers*, *Pocket Mystic: Emergency Spells*, *Pocket Mystic: Manifesting* and *Pocket Mystic: Pendulum Magic*, all also published by Quadrille.

Quadrille, Penguin Random House UK, One Embassy Gardens, 8 Viaduct
Gardens, London SW11 7BW

Quadrille Publishing Limited is part of the Penguin Random House group of
companies whose addresses can be found at global.penguinrandomhouse.com

Published by Quadrille in 2025

www.penguin.co.uk

A CIP catalogue record for this book is available from the British Library

ISBN 978-178488-983-8
10 9 8 7 6 5 4 3 2 1

Publishing Director: Kate Pollard
Editor: Phoebe Bath
Design and Art Direction: Evi-O.Studio | Katherine Zhang
Production Controller: Martina Georgieva

Colour reproduction by p2d

Printed in China by RR Donnelley Asia Printing Solution Limited

The authorised representative in the EEA is Penguin Random House Ireland,
Morrison Chambers, 32 Nassau Street, Dublin D02 YH68.

Penguin Random House is committed to a sustainable future for our business,
our readers and our planet. This book is made from Forest Stewardship Council®
certified paper.